Wild Strawberries

Anne E. Owens

....

Wild Strawberries

poems and drawings

MB
Modern Barbarian Press
Poznań, PL / Urbana, IL

Wild Strawberries
by Anne E. Owens © 2010.

Published by Modern Barbarian Press, Poznań, Poland and Urbana, Illinois.

For information on other Modern Barbarian Press publications see http://www.cafepress.com/modernbarbarian
Designed and edited by Jack J. Hutchens and Jacqueline S. Hutchens
Cover illustration by Anne E. Owens "Wild Strawberries"
Cover designed by Jack J. Hutchens and Sarah Bial

ISBN 10 - 0979123615
ISBN 13 - 9780979123610

Contents

Dedication vii

Poems 1

Goldenrod 2
Night Lights 4
When Spring Came 5
Ode to Wealth 7
Summer is 9
Evening 12
To the Fair Iris 13
Wild Strawberries 14
Let it Be 15
Blizzard 15
Winter's Grip 16
Christmas at Country Grandma's 16
Autumn's Matinée 17
Son of Mine 18
Summer 19
Wanted Peace of Mind 20
To My Missing Child 21
Winter is 22
Despair 25
Leaves of Autumn 26
Summer Storm 27
When I Retire 28
Grandma's Storm Cellar 30
How True 31
Ode to Time Passing 32
Dude's Ride 34
Old Man 35

Drawings 37

List of Illustrations

Goldenrod 3
Birdhouse 6
Sunflower 11
Campfire 12
Irises 13
Wild Strawberries 14
Pumpkin Patch 17
Sunset 18
Mountain Pines 24
Leaf 26
Clock 33
Hourglass 33
Cowboy Boot 34

About the Author 51

Dedication
To my husband Jimmy
In Memoriam
1928-1997

Whose passing has left a hole in my heart so big that only he could ever fill it. Even so, his illusive, unseen presence fills my senses and inspires me still; for memories are gifts from God that time or space cannot destroy. They wash over me in waves of indescribable joy, and I am a child again — with a brand new toy.

Goldenrod

Nodding by the dusty roadside
the lustrous goldenrod abound.
Beauteous boughs of Autumn's pride
bend heavily to the ground.

Shining in the noonday heat
swaying to the wayward breeze
for Autumn's days are short and fleet
A riot of color before the freeze.

Glowing chalices brim at sunset
Wondrous beauty to behold
As summer pays a bonus
In shimmering precious gold

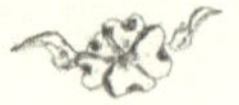

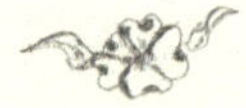

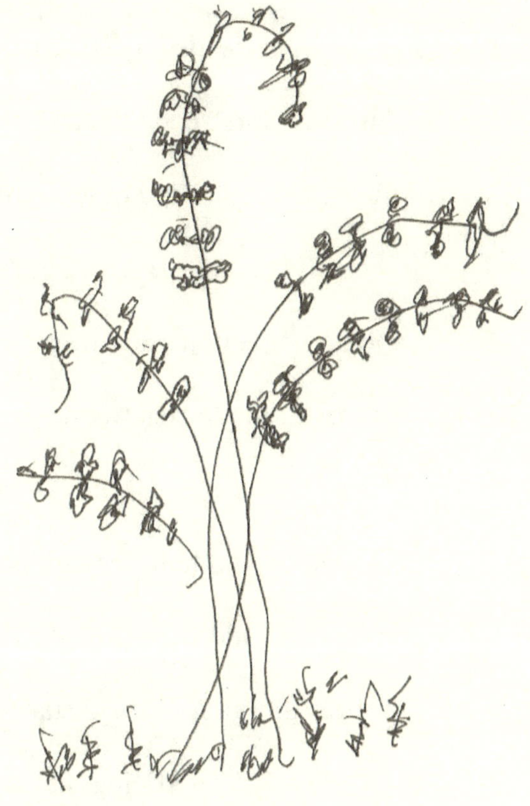

"the lustrous goldenrod abound"

Night Lights

Stars wink in the deepness above

flashing Morse code to earth

fireflies poke holes of amber light

in the velvet blanket of the night

anon a golden moon will rise

to spark the fairies wands

Street lamps twinkle in rosy globes

and lanterns add their oily glow

campfires glimmer in the distance

candles flicker on dining tables

part of nocturnes fairyland

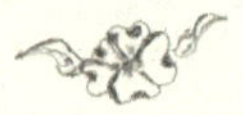

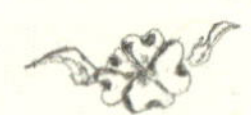

When Spring Came

Spring came gamboling o'er the shimmering green meadows
like fluffy lambs at play
Tiny flowers tossed off their blankets and jumped up on their heads
Fruit trees stretched their limbs and put hats of blossoms on their heads
Brazen tulips raised their jewel-toned goblets to the warming skies
For refills of sunbeam cocktails
Bullfrogs in the lukewarm ponds started a throaty chorus
With their lusty chuck arum
And birds of many colors added notes from their posts in the flowering plum
Trees traded their underwear of winter brown for bright green coveralls
While the flowering shrubs changed their garb to pastel tinted gowns
Spring came while puffy clouds scampered in the azure sky
And winter weary mother earth
Let out a grateful sigh

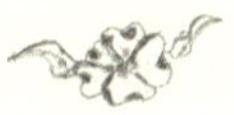

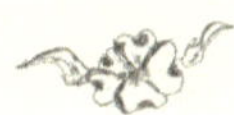

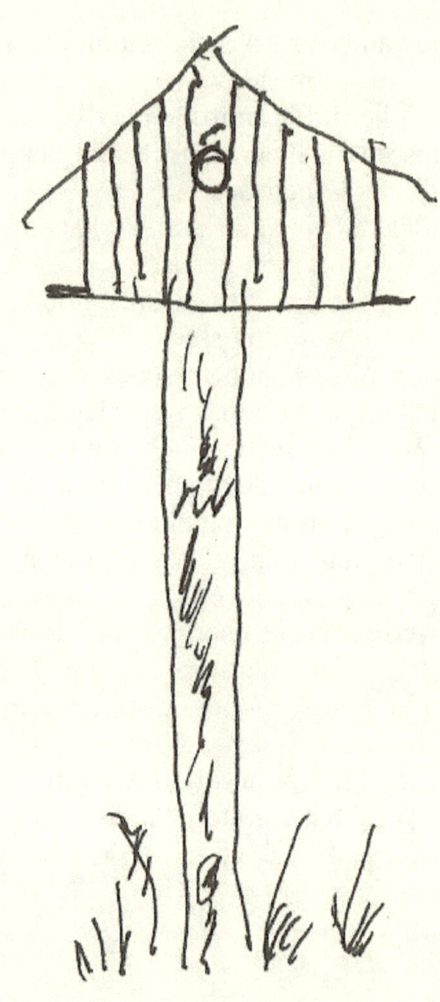

Ode To Wealth

I have no wish to amass great wealth,

for I have no desire in becoming a watchdog over it,

or a slave to it; de-sexed or dissected, because of it.

I do not want to be the target of nor envied by those

who do not have it.

I would not wish to be pushed out of shape nor

puffed up with importance by the power my dollars would command.

I would not want to question the motivation of every

gesture of friendliness or act of kindness.

I would not have money the yardstick by which

every thought word and deed is measured.

I would not like to feel I had to serve steak

when I like hamburger equally as well.

I would not wish to place my children on a velvet couch,

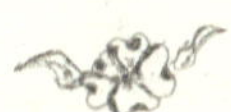

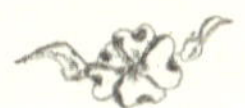

for the real world is a cactus saddle and a bucking

horse on a long long journey.

I would wish for the price of a cup of coffee in my jeans,

and enough cash to pay my obligations.

I would wish to be able to keep food on my table.

I guess I just don't wish to be poor.

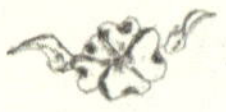

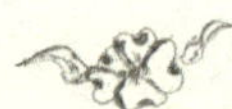

Summer Is

Summer is the frost on a pitcher of lemonade
Summer is the annual Fourth of July parade
Summer is an ice cube's tinkle
Summer is a big dill pickle
Summer is a band concert at the city park
Summer is Paris after dark
Summer is an ice cream freezer
Summer is the gay deceiver
Summer is a midnight swim
Summer is when we want to be slim
Summer is a boat under full sail
Summer is a salty gale
Summer is the Milky Way
Summer is a time to play
Summer is the county fair
Summer is the trumpet's blare
Summer is the cat's pajamas
Summer is suspense and melodramas
Summer is the creaking of a swing
Summer is the flashing redbird's wing
Summer is both this and that
Summer is a gay straw hat
Summer is a gentle breeze
Summer is some skinned up knees
Summer is a holiday grand
Summer is a ring third finger, left hand
Summer is an azure sky
Summer is a firefly
Summer is a picnic hamper
Summer is a travel camper
Summer is a fat mosquito

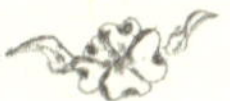

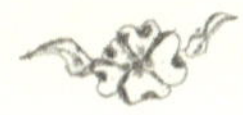

Summer is a moonlight dance
Summer is a lover's glance
Summer is creamy potato salad
Summer is a lusty ballad
Summer is a moonlight ride
Summer is a rising tide
Summer is a shady grove
Summer is a treasure trove
Summer is a ride on a merry-go-round
Summer is joy and happiness found
Summer is a bowl of strawberries
Summer is pineapple, peaches and cherries
Summer is a backyard bar-b-cue
Summer is a sudden shower or two
Summer is a field of big sunflowers
Summer is vegetable gardens and rose bowers
Summer is waves of golden grain
Summer is a speeding train
Summer is a nightingale's song
Summer is actually three months long
Summer is a time of challenge and endeavor
Summer, for me, is now and forever

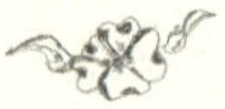

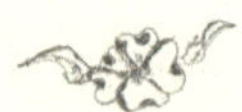

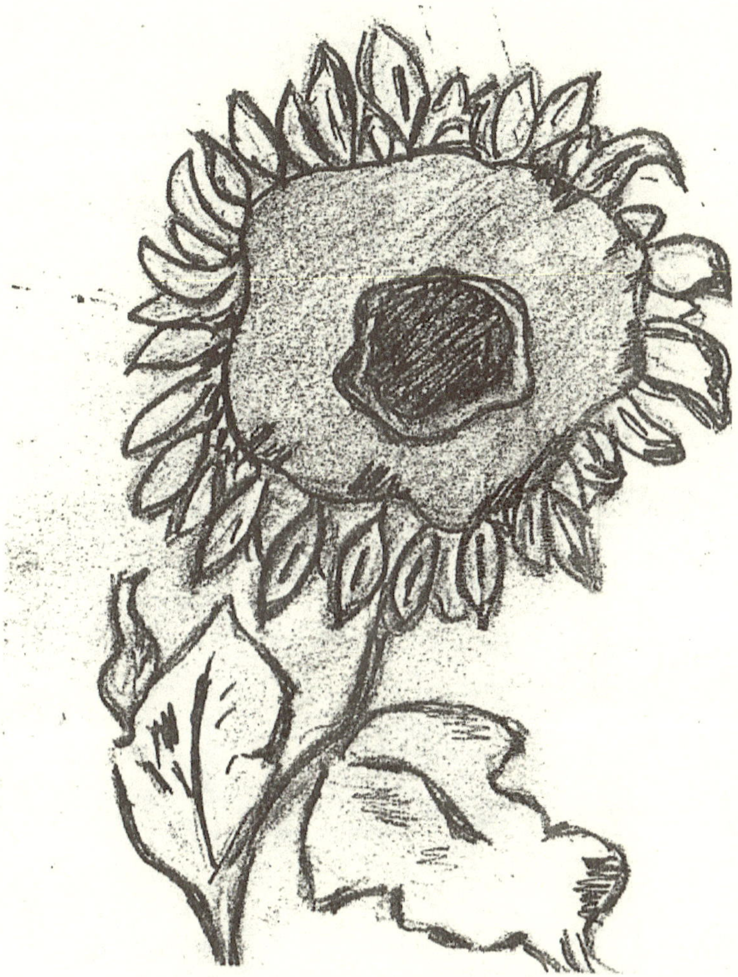

"Summer is a field of big sunflowers"

Evening

Evening draws her lavender drape
across earth's picture window
as sunny day makes it's escape
in twilights afterglow

Anon the tiny stars will twinkle
in the velvety darkness of the sky
sparkle dust on lavender drapes to sprinkle
'til dawn bids night goodbye

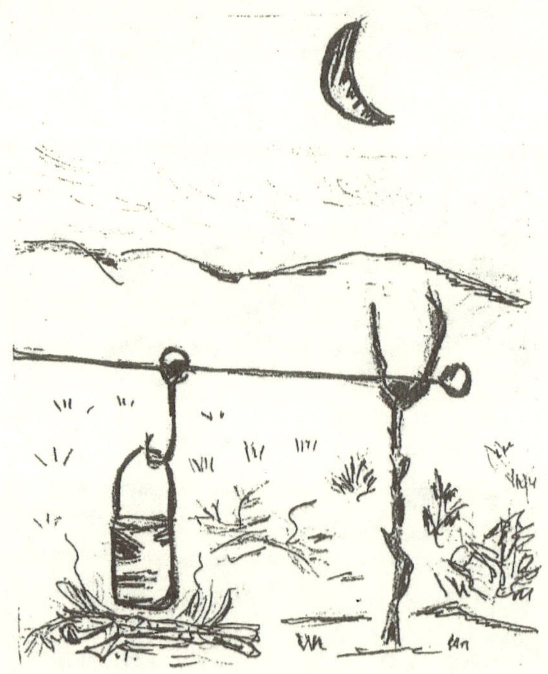

To the Fair Iris

Prima Dona of the spring
lovely iris on your regal stem
preening with your buds unfurled
fairest of the flower world
exquisite beauty of many hues
you grace the courtyard of king and peasant
dewy petals so soft and exotic
delicate scent sweetly hypnotic
semiprecious iris of the season's ballet
you hold center stage in my springtime garden

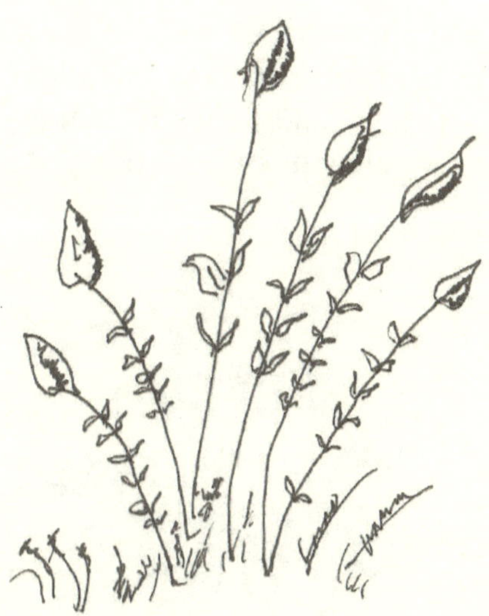

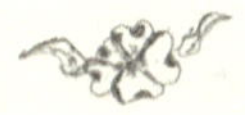

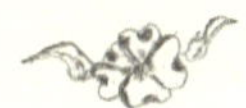

Wild Strawberries

Plump wild strawberries, ripe and juicy
nestle in the crisp emerald grass
They glow like precious rubies
flung form a gypsy's hand

With no apology for their being
nature's tart gift to man
proudly await springs harvests
ready to be eaten or canned

Anon, they will glow from glass houses
on pantry shelves row on row
jams and jellies for winter
elegant sweets so grand

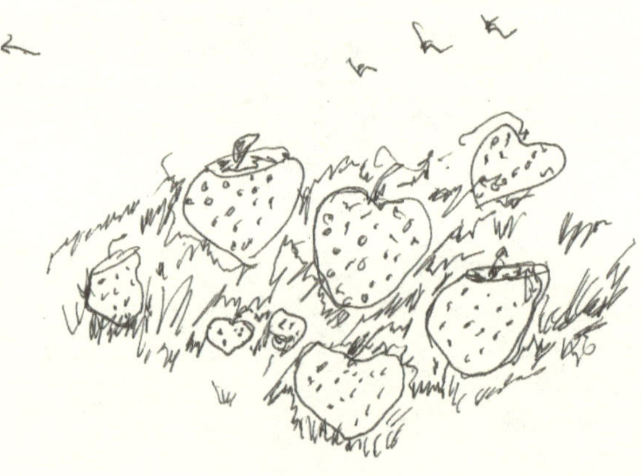

Let It Be

Let the wind blow
and the river flow
Let the sun set
and the moon rise
Let the grass grow
and the flower bloom
Let the world turn
and the stars shine
Let the merchant haggle
and the politician procrastinate
and oh lord, let every man stir his own gravy

Blizzard

Howling winds lash the earth
while a great white blanket flaps o'er the land
merciless they show no mirth
flinging snowflakes with a ruthless hand
beast or man cannot escape
the frigid icy grip
when ruthless winter flicks it's cape
and snaps it's cutting whip

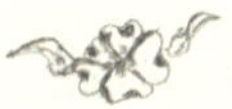

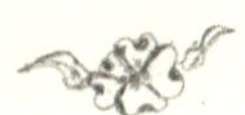

Winter's Grip

A yellow moon full and luminous
keeps watch in a frost filled sky
missing nothing that moves in the night
casting it's light on snowdrifts high

A gust of frigid air comes blasting
holding all in it's icy grip
man nor beast cannot escape
a lashing from it's frozen whip

Christmas At Country Grandma's

We chug down the narrow snow packed lane
each passing mile brings us closer
family warmth and gifts await
as we pass through the old farm gate
that leads to the white frame house
of our dear little country grandma

Inside a cheery fire will snap and blaze
to warm our fingers and toes
uncles aunts and cousins will smother us with kisses
and greet us with warm yuletide wishes
in our hearts we know that this will be
the best Christmas ever at country grandma's

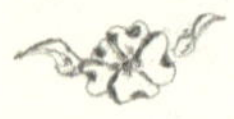

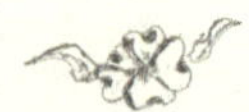

Autumn's Matinee

Corn shocks stand tall in ragged rows
at attention to the sun
Pumpkins fat and orange
are ready for Halloween's fun

Pasture lands turn dry and brown
awaiting winter's cold
swirling leaves whirl through the sky
like madcaps gay and bold

Wild geese start their journey south
and sound their sad goodbye
smoke of burning leaves ascends
in the bright October sky

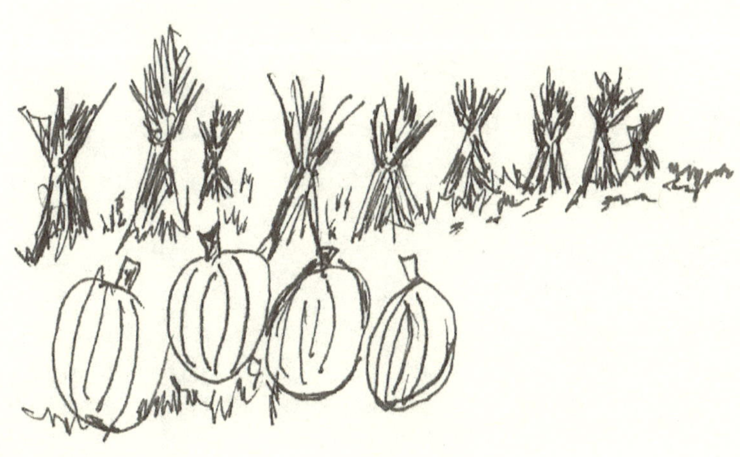

Son of Mine

Your are most precious son of mine
you fill my days with joy
A blend of angel and mischief
you darling little boy

Your needs and wants are mine to fill
as I watch you work and play
my heart will remember little son
when you're a man some day

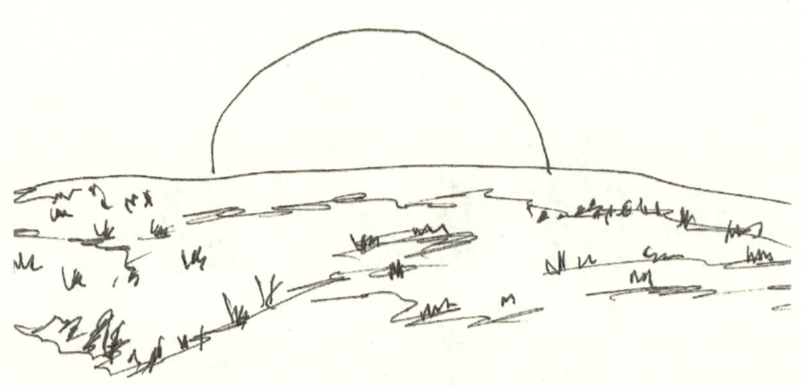

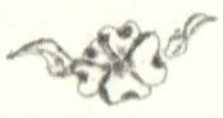

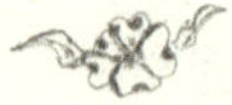

Summer

Summer flits a scarf of bright chiffon
at the gentle passing breeze
and wafts a perfume sweet and heady
as she floats among the flowering trees

Stardust glistens in her hair
and moon glow twinkles in her eyes
as she sways to music of night sounds
of tiny gauze winged insects in the skies

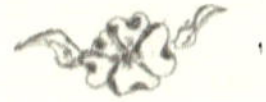

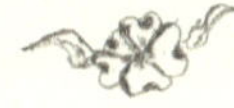

Wanted Peace of Mind

Would that I could find a place
to take a quiet stroll
where cares and troubles could not creep
and naught could pierce my soul

A scrap or bit of land
removed from stress and strain
where I could be alone
and rest my weary brain

Perhaps some secret cozy cove
along the rockbound coasts
where the quiet lapping waves
would help to lay my ghosts

A quiet secluded bower
somewhere on God's green Earth
where I could drift and dream
and comprehend my worth

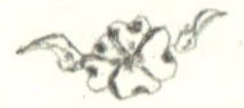

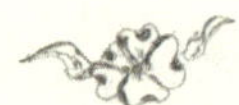

To My Missing Child

Out of the night my heart cries for you
anguish untold twists me apart
from the depths of my agony
hear my tortured call
o'er hill and dale my pleading cries fall

My heart is sad-twisted-torn
grief comes and stays
an unwelcomed guest
nothing but dull black pain ahead
the child of my heart has fled
I knew not of your deepest thoughts
or problems that you pondered
I could not fathom your secret desires
that pressure often inspires

My soul cannot rest
until you return
send me a word -a sign-
a message to say you are safe
that you are found my wandering waif

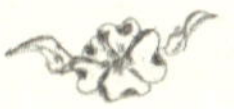

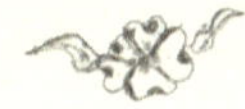

Winter Is

Winter is a cozy fireside
Winter is a bobsled ride
Winter is a breath of icy air
Winter is a grizzly bear
Winter is an interlude
Winter is summer in the nude
Winter is the morning star
Winter is a balky car
Winter is a long icicle
Winter is a season fickle
Winter is a big red mitten
Winter is a nose frostbitten
Winter is a red stocking cap
Winter is a warm woolly wrap
Winter is the time your furnace overheats
Winter is time to read Shelly, Brown and Keats
Winter is a leaping flame
Winter is a checker game
Winter is a chestnut roasting
Winter is some marshmallows toasting
Winter is a flighty fellow
Winter is a silvery cello
Winter is ice and snow and sleet
Winter is a lost lambs bleat
Winter is cream of wheat and oatmeal
Winter is tangy lemon and orange peel
Winter is a pot of chocolate steaming
Winter is a time for dreaming
Winter is a ten-pound fruitcake

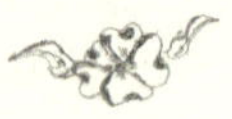

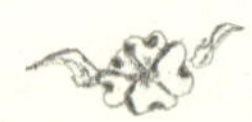

Winter is a coffee break
Winter is a glittering fairyland
Winter is a wedding band
Winter is the harbinger of spring
Winter is a snowbirds wing
Winter is Christmas lights that twinkle
Winter is bows and ribbons that crinkle
Winter is a child's stocking hung
Winter is carols being sung
Winter is when Santa comes
Winter is plum pudding and sugarplums
Winter is the last verse of the calendars season
Winter is the answer to summer's treason

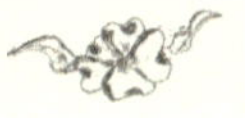

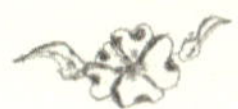

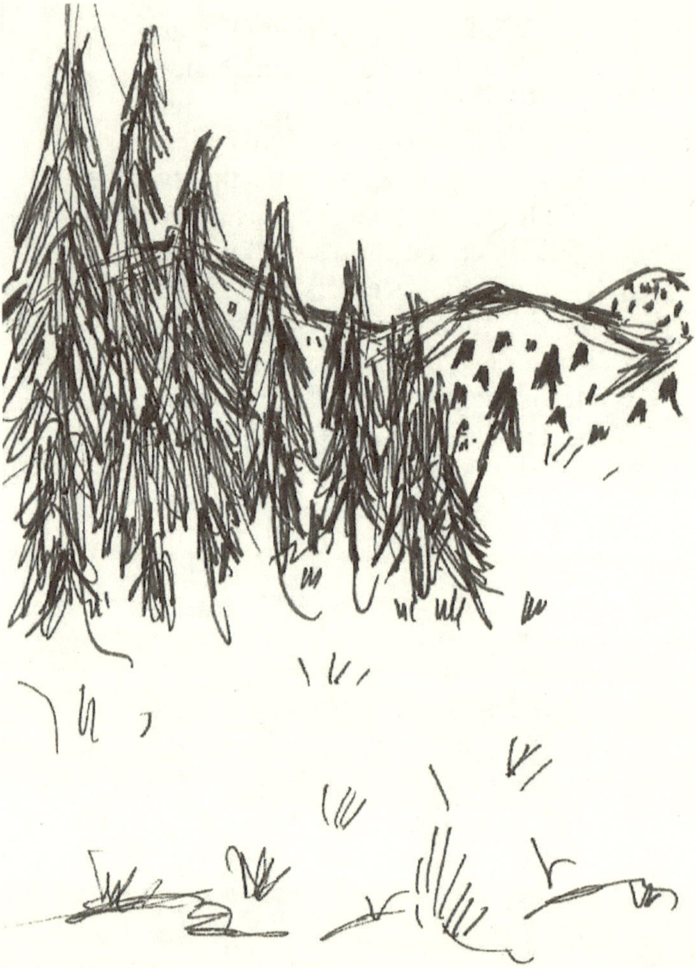

Despair

Endless night of lurking shadows
draped in ebony folds of nothingness
Requiem of dreams unborn
dash all hopes with frowns of scorn
aspirations bleak and barren
condemn the future null and void
vital forces fighting dawn
unproductive weak and wan
lacrimation mixed with ashes
from a mud of desolation
spirit questions it's existence
in its hell finds no resistance
heart that beats a steady dirge
pulse finds no excuse to surge
crushing arms of dull dark night
push tomorrow out of sight

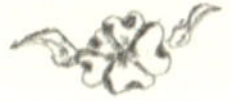

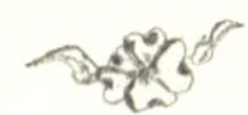

Leaves of Autumn

Leaves of yellow orange and umber
scamper and scurry through the air
swirling twirling at their play
branches of their tree house bare

Leaves of nutmeg gold and crimson
float to earth in leisurely style
en masse is the wood
soon they'll meet a color riot to beguile

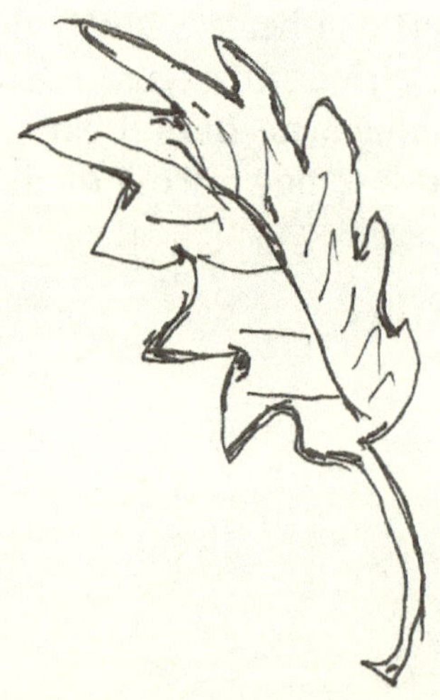

Summer Storm

Dark clouds rendezvous on far horizons
like armies reconnoitering for an attack
their faces dark with unspent fury
and bulging muscles glistening ebony black

Summer blows its' sultry breath upon the weary land
parching everything unmindful of our needs
and perspiration swathes us
in salty rolling beads.

Lightning fingers answer the insult
and slap the face of summer
with shafts of blinding fury
like an anti-aircraft gunner

Thunder bawls across the tortured earth
a repetitious note relayed
that soon the precious rain will fall
for which the farmers prayed.

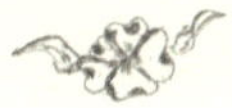

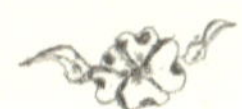

When I Retire

When I retire from my chosen work
and look at pastures new
I'll lay away the precious past
In folds of tissue blue

I do not aim to bar the door
On days and years so dear
I merely seek to walk new paths
And work in slower gear

There's been a lot of sad dark days
Shuffled with the good
I wouldn't trade a single moment
Not even if I could

I had those good productive years
I lived them one day at a time
I filled them to the very brim
They were a heady wine

Yes I have tasted from the bitter cup
but I've chased it with the sweet
And I suppose a lump of lowly clay
Was used to mold my feet

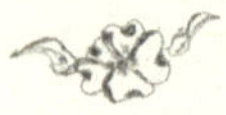

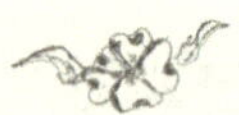

I've made a lot of errors
I'm not ashamed to say
But there was always tomorrow
And I tried again another day

After I have seen the sights
And visited friends so pleasant
I'll take the memories from tissue blue
And tuck them in with the present

I'll face the future brave and honest
Without regret or dread
There simply isn't time for tears
There's too much up ahead

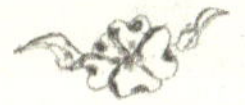

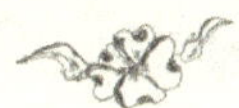

Grandma's Storm Cellar

Haven in the bowels of earth
reached by stone steps worn smooth by use
there we fled to reach quick shelter
when twisters threatened and raindrops would pelt
we slammed the heavy sloped wood door
that sealed us from the fury of the world outside
down the dark narrow passage—fast as our legs could carry
we groped our way in the cozy gloom of that stone-lined
sanctuary
we shivered feeling smug—yet oh so humble
knowing we'd won a race with the elements
there in a niche—where we knew it would be
the trusty kerosene lantern we lit so we could see
rays of pale yellow light dispelled the shadows
as we kids took quick inventory of all we surveyed
stone crocks of cream not quite sweet
pints and quarts of the spicy red beet
stalks of dill strung from the ceiling
wafted a piquant aroma
baskets of apples sassy and red
jars of starter Grandma used to bake bread
potatoes paraded in rows on newspapers
carrots basked in shallow wood boxes
shelves lined with jars of watermelon pickle
green beans, corn and mincemeat for the fickle
a green melon floated in a big wooden tub
a treat some evening of a hot day's harvest

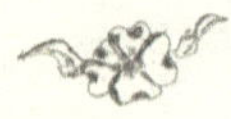

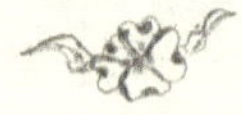

cucumbers in brine and tins of lard
bars of lye soap white and hard
glasses of jams, preserves and jellies
quarts of plums, peaches and pears to treat us all winter
jelled canned beef and strings of wurst
we kids would eat 'till we thought we'd burst
wondrous delight the memories of our childhood
the treasures we beheld in Grandma's storm cellar

How True

A man will stand for just so much
e'er he's tempted to add his touch

Upon his assailant standing there
with blows to the head or yank to the hair

It matters not if act or word
the outrage ne'er the less is heard

Whether it's a verbal form of assault
or physical contact that's at fault

Man must render a sharp retort
even if it means his "day in court"

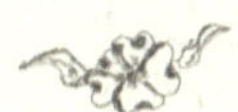

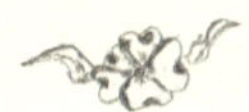

Ode To Time Passing

Would that I could extend the swiftly passing hours
and apprehend the sands of time
suspending each tiny grain in timeless incarceration.
I would surely arrest the precious swift illusive seconds
as they scamper by on winged feet
in headlong pursuit of eternity
and hold them to me in eager appreciative arms
realizing my treasure I would savor
the heady wine of leisure
and sense the healing balm of solitude
my heart would flutter its gossamer wings in expectation
upon the doors of contentment
while minutes advancing from antiquity ceased their
ticking
but alas and anon the irretrievable particles
of my finite existence journey into infinity
severing the illusive hold which I claim for my own
echoing on the winds I hear time whisper
by me chanting its immortal refrain
catch me catch me if you can
truly, truly I cannot wait for any man.

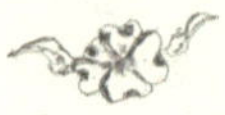

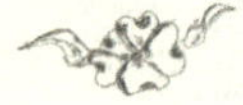

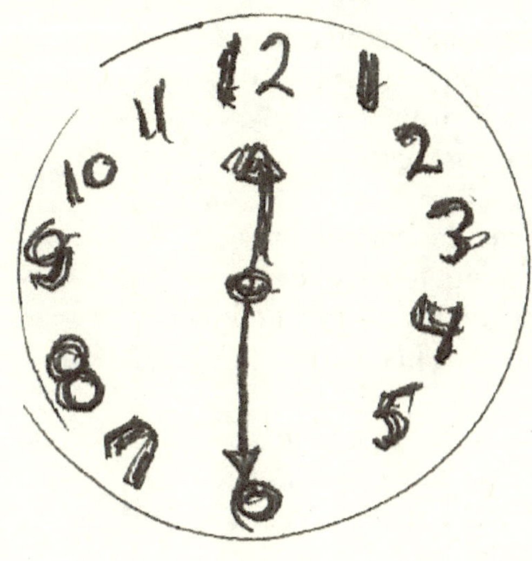
12
1
2
3
4
5
6
7
8
9
10
11

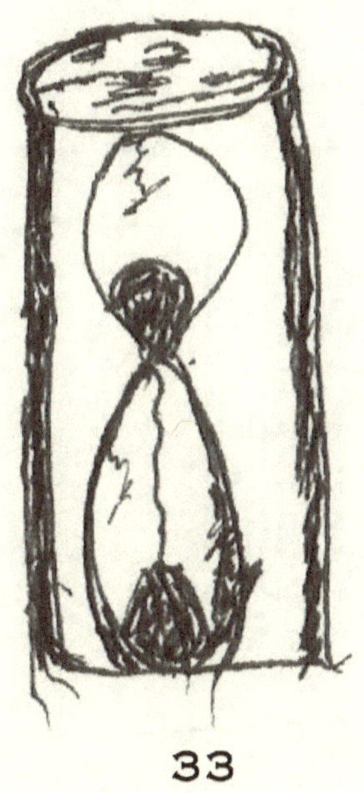

Dude's Ride

Night will find me on the trail
by my fire red and cheery,
resting in my bedroll
for I am growing weary.

I'll take the saddle from my horse
and stake him out to pasture,
I'll feed him good and rub him down
for he's as tired as his master.

A fire hot and a pot of coffee
will put me in a better mood,
some bacon and a plate of beans
will really help this dude.

After I have ate a bite
and smoked a pipe or two,
I'll crawl into my bedroll
and dream of the west when it was new.

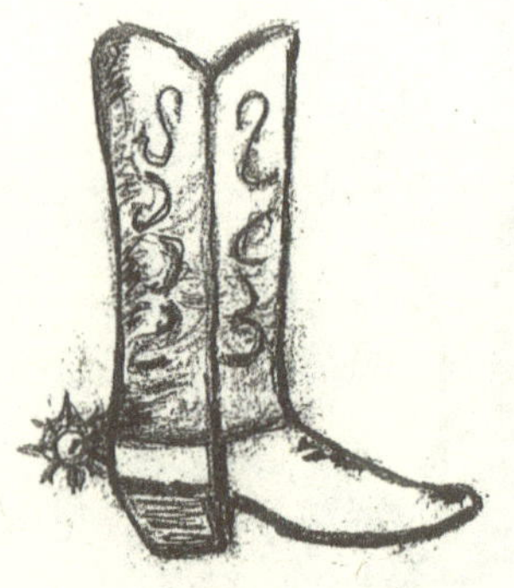

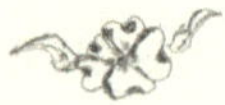

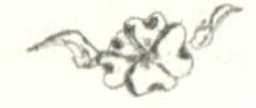

Old Man

Old man you stand there quite unnoticed
on life's bustling sidewalks
quiet small and unobtrusive
left alone with thoughts exclusive
totally ignored by those rushing past you.

Once you stood among the leaders
planning, toiling, dreaming, doing
called upon for help and advise
no job too big, you could pay the price.
When you spoke your voice held authority
you commanded respect and admiration.

Old man what's the strange light in you eye?
Is it a reflection of happier times?
You have wealth more precious than any gold
if your experiences were told
put your stories into words on paper
youth will be more tolerant when they've read it

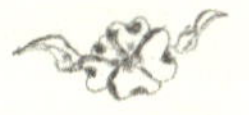

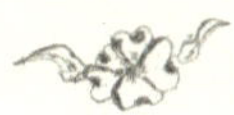

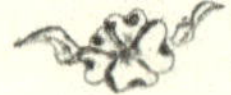

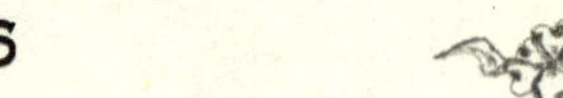

Drawings

Bouquet....................38

Campfire....................39

Grapes....................40

Homestead....................41

Pasture....................42

Bluebells....................43

Scarecrow....................44

Windmill....................45

Windmill No. 2....................46

Potatoes....................47

Lighthouse....................48

Wheat Shock....................49

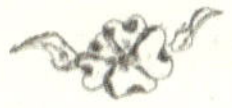

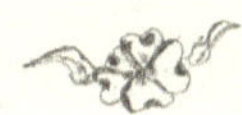

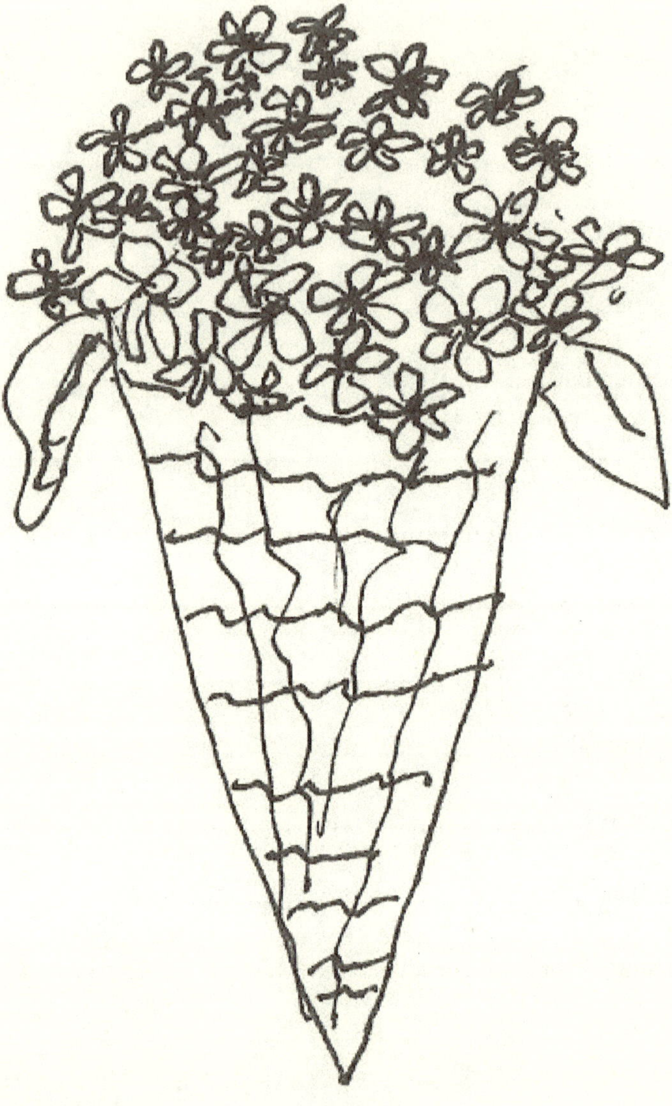

"Bouquet"

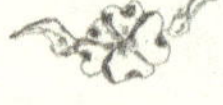

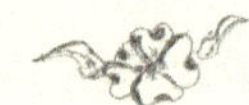

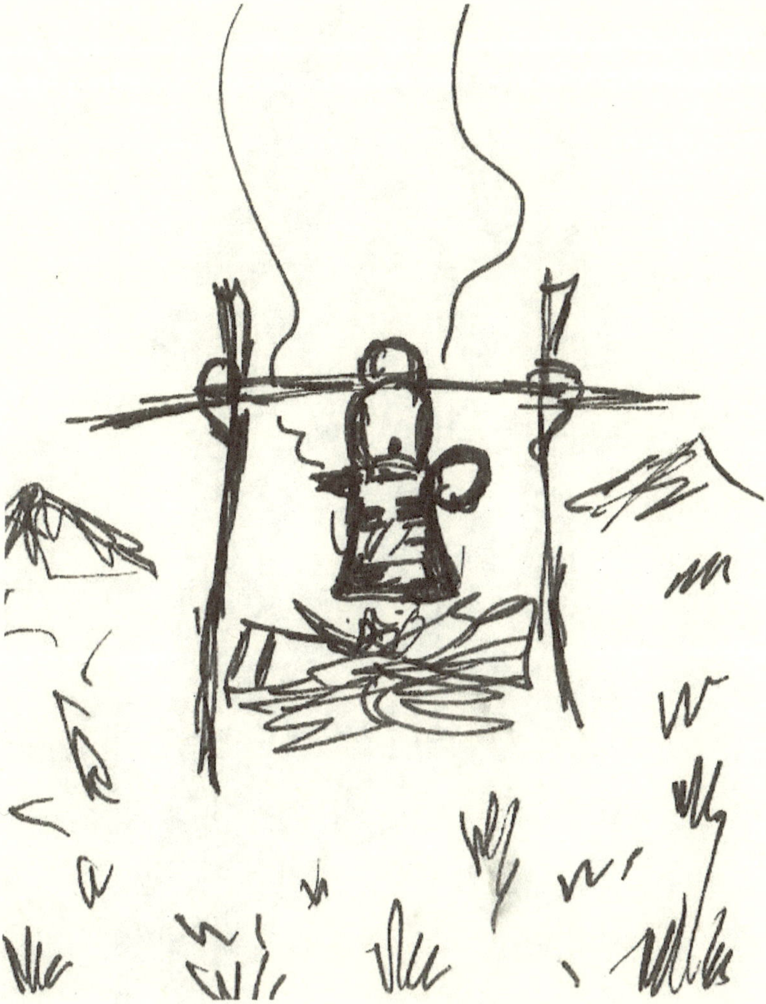

"*Campfire*"

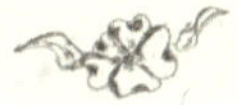

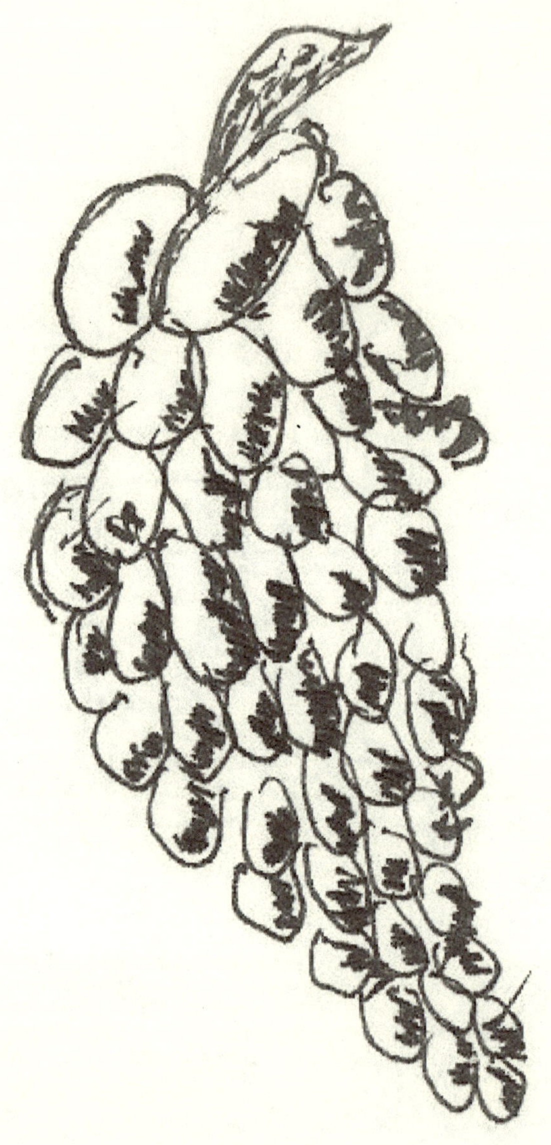

"Grapes"

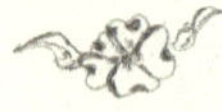

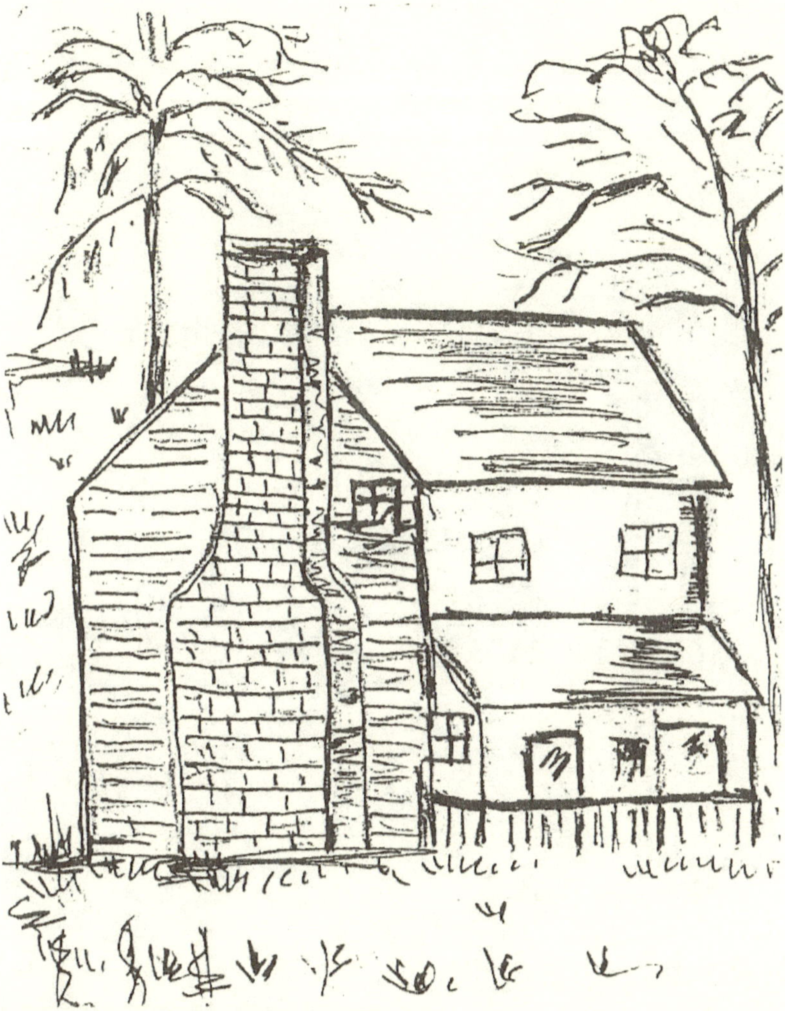

"Homestead"

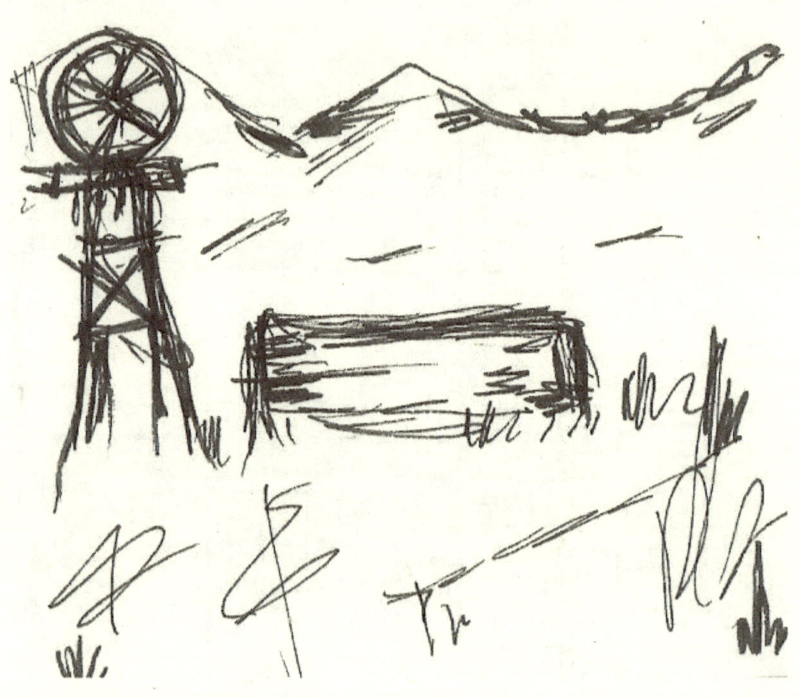

"Pasture"

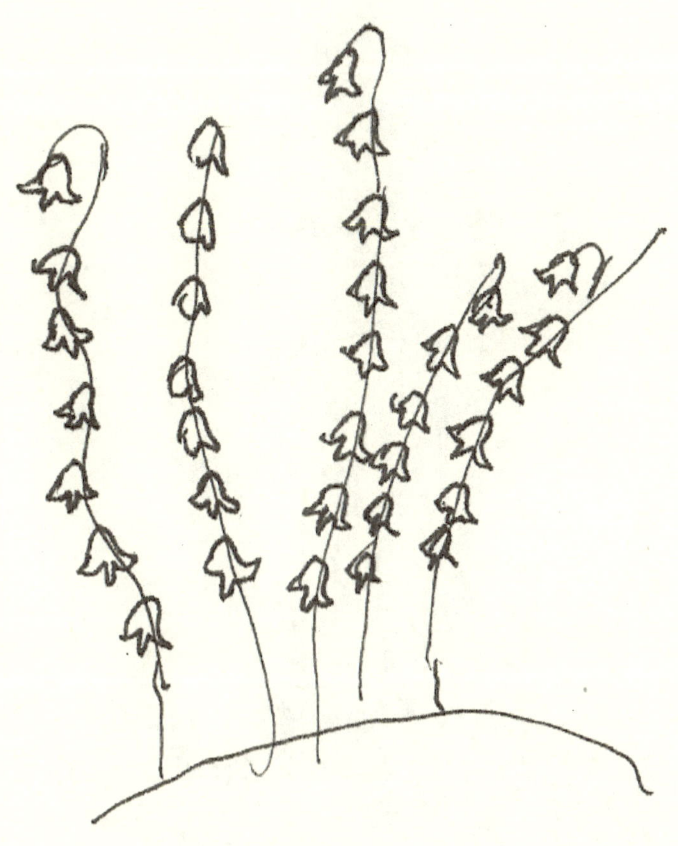

"Bluebells"

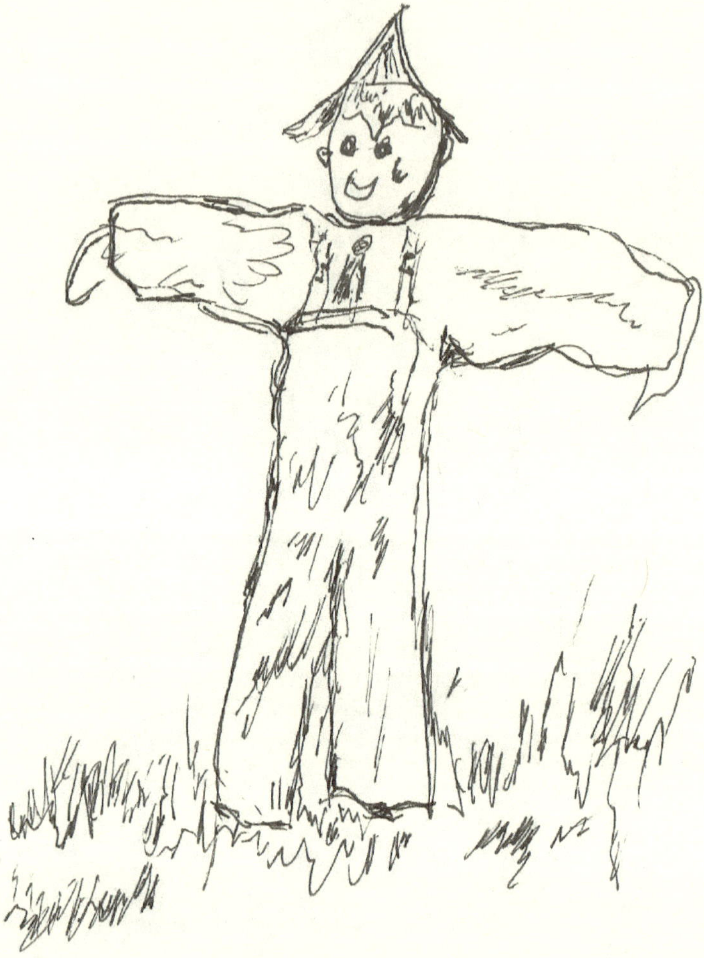

"Scarecrow"

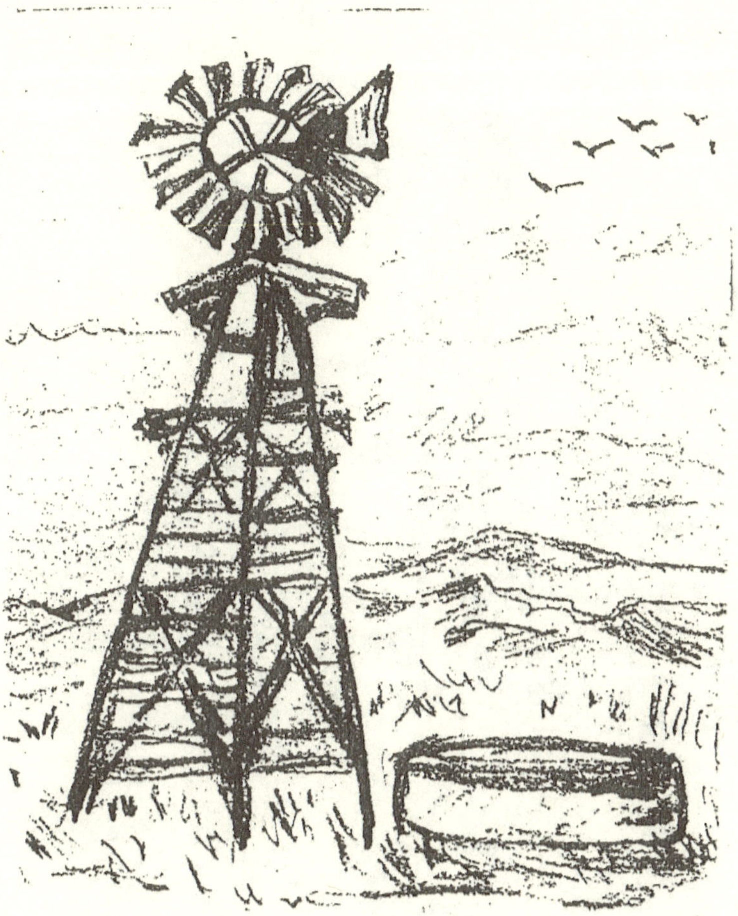

"Windmill"

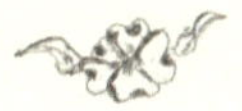

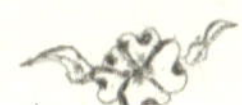

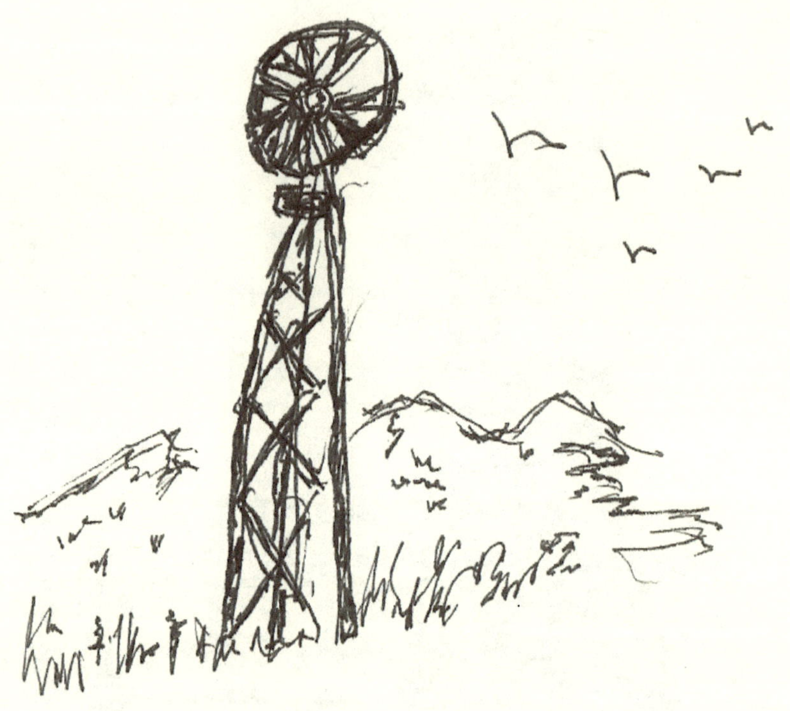

"Windmill No. 2"

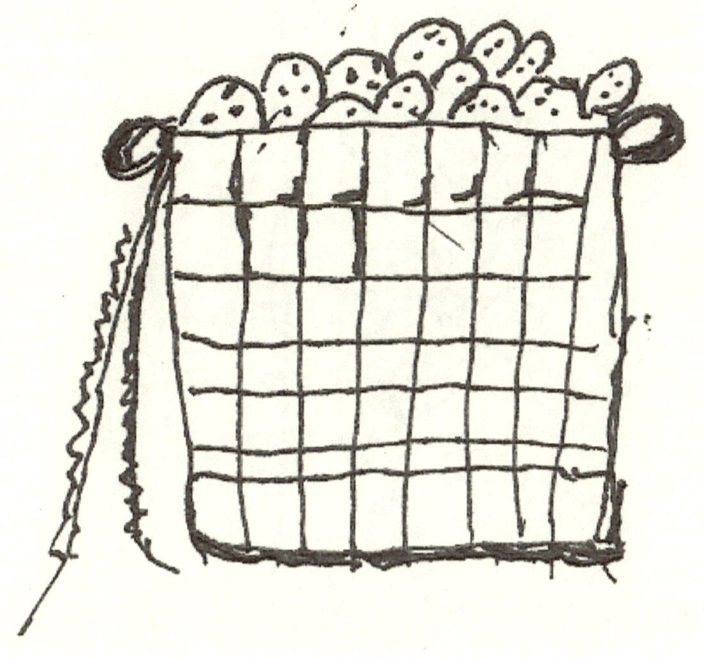

"Potatoes"

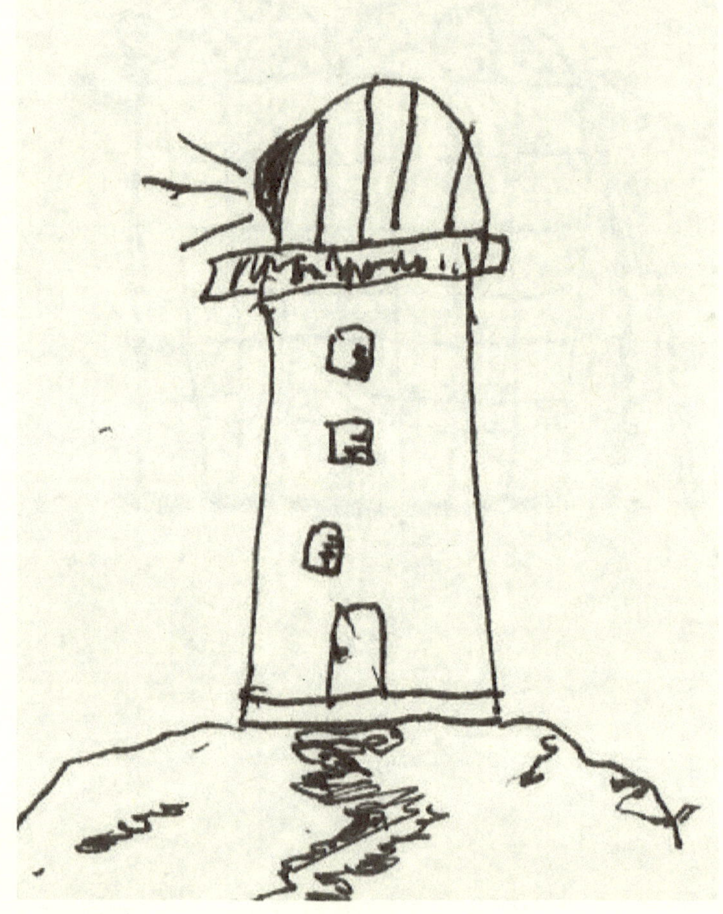

"Lighthouse"

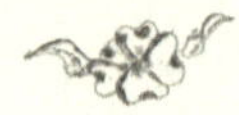

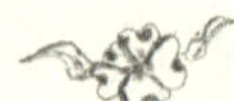

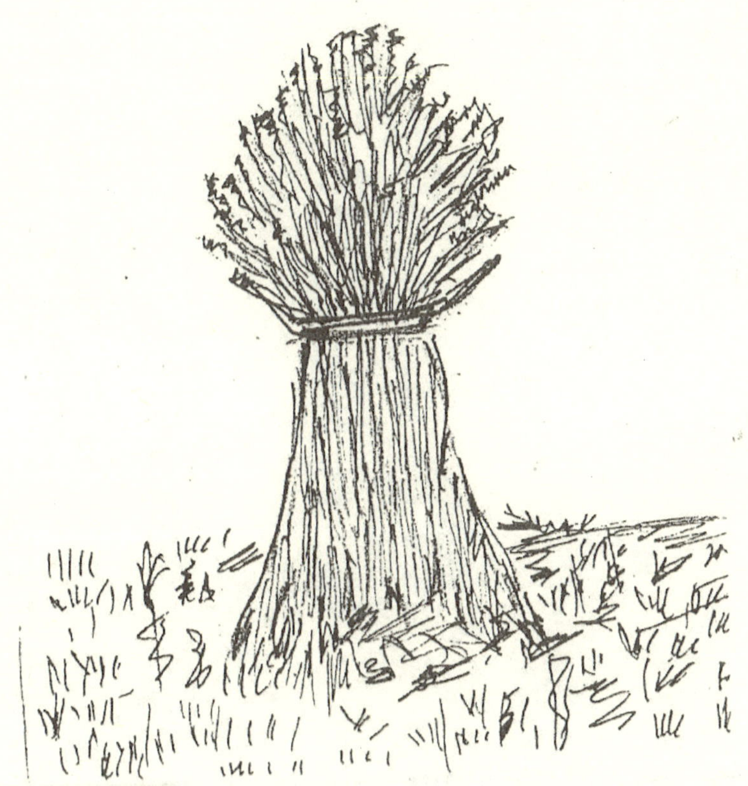

"Wheat Shock"

About the author

Anne E. Owens, a native Kansan, made her debut on the stage of life at LaCross, Kansas in Rush County, on September 23,1928. She arrived just in time for "Dust Bowl Days" of the infamous Dirty Thirties. Her friends know her as "Annie." She tells of how she was on her way to a picnic the day she was born and that she has been on a picnic ever since. Her parents were en route to a picnic at Lake Barton near Great Bed, Kansas when Annie decided she just couldn't wait even one more day to get acquainted. They left posthaste for home. There in a state of utter confusion and excitement, Annie met her dad, Jack, a handsome young Irishman, and Anna, her pretty Volga-German mother. It was the first day of Autumn. Annie grew up in the western Kansas oil patch, where her dad worked. The family lived in various towns during the big oil boom. She attended high school during World War Two, and graduated from Great Bend Senior High. She met and married her husband Jimmy, a Navy Airman and WW2 veteran, in 1950. He died on September 12, 1997 on the seventeenth anniversary of her mother's death. There are three children and 8 grandchildren (four are living), and 8 great grand children.

Annie has worked at many jobs and worn many hats. She has been an American Red Cross volunteer, assigned to Collmery-O'neill Veteran's Hospital in Topeka, Kansas. She was a vocalist and production manager for a country and western band, and operated a wrecker in a salvage yard. She ran her shop, Country Annie's, a Country-Folk-

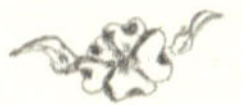

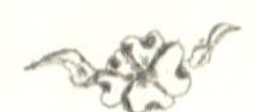

Primitive-Victorian business, in a vintage bank for nine years. She holds the distinct honor of being the first woman to graduate from Manhattan, Kansas Law Enforcement Officers' Training School, class of 1972. She was employed by the Wabaunsee County sheriff's department for 6 years. She was the first woman law enforcement officer for the county, and the first official dispatcher for the 791 square mile territory. A deputy sheriff, she was partnered with her husband, Under Sheriff Jim "Rocky" Owens.

Currently she is working on a non-fiction book, and writes nature essays. She is an artist and poet. She oversees the job of redecorating the interior of her 19th century one room stone schoolhouse and plans to landscape the 5-acre tract it sets on. She tends perennial flowerbeds at her home at "Raccoon Run" near Eskridge, Kansas where she has resided for the past 50 years. In idle moments she studies geography and reads history.

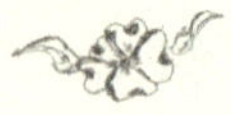

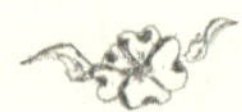

www.ingramcontent.com/pod-product-compliance
Lightning Source LLC
LaVergne TN
LVHW050945080826
845145LV00004B/1415

* 9 7 8 0 9 7 9 1 2 3 6 1 0 *